4 Months
The prequel to 52 Weeks

Barry Lillie

Copyright © Barry Lillie 2024

Cover design © Flatfield

The moral right of Barry Lillie to be identified as the author of this work has been asserted in accordance with the Copyright, Designs and Patents Act of 1988.

All rights reserved. No part of this publication may be reproduced, stored in a retrieval system, or transmitted in any form or by any means, electronic, mechanical, photocopying, recording, or otherwise, without the prior permission of the copyright owner of this book.

This novel is entirely a work of fiction. The names, characters and incidents portrayed within are the product of the author's imagination. Any resemblance to actual people living or dead is entirely coincidental.

You can follow Barry on the following platforms:
www.barrylillie.com
www.facebook.com/barrylillieauthor
www.instagram.com/barrylillie2

For news about new releases and free content sign up for Barry's Book Club mailing list.

1. Doreen's New Carpet

Friday 5 March 1982
Today, Donna volunteered to fetch the breakfast orders, The seventeen-year-old trainee is desperate to show off her new hairdo. She's become a fan of the new wave band, Bow Wow Wow and so today sported a Mohican cut just like the lead singer. However, Donna's head shape is not as aesthetically pleasing as Annabella Lwin's and sadly the baldness makes it obvious that her left ear is much higher than the right.

"Thanks for this, Donna," Vera says receiving her breakfast. "Bet you can feel the cold now half your hair's on the hairdresser's floor."

"You bet, and for some reason, me specs keep sliding off, now there's no hair to hold them in place," Donna laughed; well half snorted and half laughed before delivering the remaining breakfasts further down the line.

"What you had Beryl?"

"Sausage and cheese, what about you?" I don't know why I bothered asking as it was obvious Vera had had egg as she'd got a long line of yellow yolk running down her chin and onto the front of her overall.

There's ten of us on our line, all girls – we're known as girls but our ages range from seventeen to fifty-three. Cup handlers we are and it's our job to fit the handles onto the clay cups and sponge off the mould marks. It's a good job, not mentally taxing but this means we can have a good gossip as we work and the radio's always on, so we get to hear the latest pop songs and have a sing-along if we like. The current favourite is 'Mickey' by Toni Basil, where in the pop video, Ms Basil is dressed as an American cheerleader. Some of the girls in the glost warehouse were trying to recreate the video and after clambering on someone's shoulders one of them fell and knocked over a trolley stacked with teapots, although no one owned up, they'd smashed two days' worth of work and the management banned everyone from singing along with the song.

Breakfast is over, and Andrew, our section manager comes around to send the girls from other departments back to their places. After wiping down her overall, Vera returns to her job as a biscuit selector and, Margaret goes back to the lithographing benches upstairs. "How's the little one, Beryl?"

"He's doing well thanks," I tell Andrew, "doctor says it was just a touch of croup."

"Pleased to hear it."

That's how it is on a potbank, and I can't see ours being much different than any of the others in the city. Everyone's friendly, we're like one big family; everyone knows everyone's business. We all come from similar households3, most of us have been working in the pots ever since we left school. I've been at this place for 12 years; I did four years at another factory first but I'm settled here now.

I met my husband, Len here, he's a handle caster working in the clay end. He started chatting to me one day when he helped the labourers bring some fresh handles to our benches, and we've been together ever since. We've been married 16 years, so we're not love's young dream, but we get by. Like most of the people working here, husbands and wives work for the same potbank and later their children often follow in their footsteps, the pottery industry is, you could say, a family thing.

***

The weather's fine today so we've decided to take our lunchboxes outside and sit on the wall. Ricky Ross, a new labourer working in clay end has caught the eye of some of the girls, and he's subjected daily to wolf whistles and lewd comments as he pushes his barrow of clay back to the slip house. "Take your top off Ricky," Patricia shouts, "Give us a flash of your ginger pits."

"Leave him alone," Vera says.

"It's just a bit of fun Vee," Stella Murphy says, "Mind you, looking at him he needs a good feed, If you found him in bed with you, you'd think someone had lost a pair of tights."

"Just imagine Ricky in the buff with his ginger bush," Donna says pulling a face.

"Oh no!" Margaret says, "His do-dah would look like a sleeping dormouse." We all turn around just in time to see Ricky flash the V sign before he disappears inside the slip house.

Sitting in a haze of cigarette smoke, some of the girls are flicking through the Freemans catalogue, choosing what outfits they'll be buying in weekly instalments. "Hey Beryl, what do you think of this?" I look around and Stella's holding up a picture of a batwing top in yellow. "I might get this for Kathleen's engagement party."

"Bit bright isn't it?"

"That's the whole point, it's 1982 not 1952."

"Yeah, neon is in, now," Donna says, pushing her glasses back up her nose.

"I thought you were a punk rocker," Vera shouts over.

"Not a punk, I'm into new wave and we embrace other types of music too."

"Oh, get you, the experienced impresario."

"Impre-what?"

"What are you getting for Kathleen's bottom drawer?" Stella continues.

"Not sure, Len said as it's her third engagement I'm not to spend too much. He reckons she'll have enough stuff to fill a wardrobe by now."

"Third engagement and she's only just gone twenty."

"Too eager to settle down, that one is," Patricia says.

"I'm thinking of getting a leopard skin mini to wear at the party," Donna adds to the conversation.

"With that hairstyle, all you need to complete the outfit is a bow and arrow."

"Ha bloody ha, Vera, what you going to wear eh? A frilly frock like Princess Di?" Donna says.

"If it's good enough for our future queen it's good enough for me."

The buzzer sounds and cigarettes are stubbed out on the wall and Tupperware lids are replaced. "Come along girls," Andrew calls as we enter the building, "Dinner break was over two minutes' ago." We all shuffle back to our benches, stopping at the sinks first to fetch clean water for our afternoon shift of sponging the seams off handles.

"I'm thinking of getting her a toaster, they've some nice ones with ears of wheat on them in the catalogue," Stella says as she perfectly applies a handle without looking.

"What you on about?" I ask her.

"For Kathleen's bottom drawer."

Not this again, I think. "Len said she ought to be happy with a cruet set from the market."

"Do you think she's ever returned the last two engagement rings she got given?"

"I know her mother wears one of them now," I reply.

"She's always been a bit of a mummy's girl has Kathleen."

"Tell me about it, they're so close you'd be hard-pressed to slip a buttered knife between them."

The familiar sound of wheels on concrete indicates the labourers' have arrived to pick up clay waste, Ricky stops at our line and is collecting the buckets of broken handles from beneath the benches when Donna says, "Here he is … Hey Ricky, have you got a girlfriend, or just in a deep relationship with your right hand?"

"Leave the lad alone Donna," Andrew shouts from across the room.

"It's just a laugh."

"The only laugh around here is you," Ricky says, "With that stupid haircut and specs, you look like a short-sighted parrakeet." Donna blushes, the pink rising right up above her ears to her shaved hairline and everyone bursts out laughing before singing, 'Go Wild in the Country.' Ricky saunters off grinning, he's won this battle, but not the war. The poor lad has got to come back again before the shift ends.

***

At the end of each day, the streets are filled with pottery workers walking home, men covered in clay dust and women with grey slip under their fingernails. It seems like everyone working at the potbank lives close enough to walk home and only a handful of the 'girls' I work with use the reliable bus services.

Our house is just ten minutes away and I'm walking home with Vera when she reminds me that we've promised to visit Doreen tonight to look at her new carpet.

"I'd forgotten."

"I'd rather not to be honest," Vera says, "If it wasn't for Mavis I wouldn't bother with her, she's so critical she makes Maggie Thatcher look like a liberal.

"She's not that bad."

"Come on Beryl, she's as severe as her plucked eyebrows." When we reach Vera's, she opens her front door and says, "I'll call for you at seven."

My next stop on my journey is to Mavis, she's home all day and so looks after Victor my three-year-old, and later, collects Lisa my six-year-old daughter from school, looking after the two of them until I finish work. It's been a good arrangement as Mavis not only looks like the epitome of a childcare specialist; rounded edges and a smile that never falters at the corners, she's softly spoken and generous to a fault. I press the doorbell and I can hear my daughter shouting as she runs down the passage to the front door with Mavis behind telling her to be careful. It's the same routine every evening. Lisa is so excitable, always a handful. I once told Len she'd grow up headstrong, and his reply was, she'll be a woman who'll need a strong husband.

"Come in duck," Mavis says around the door, shall I put the kettle on?"

"That'll be lovely." I step inside and Lisa is trying to tell me all about her day at school, "We made nature crowns today, I put ladybirds on mine." At that point, Victor walks into the hallway wearing a hat made up of paper leaves with a large, red-spotted beetle on the side.

"Hello little fella," I say bending to pick him up. He nuzzles into my chest with a wide smile plastered across his face. Unlike his sister, Victor's less robust, he's a quiet little boy, happy to take cuddles from his mother, whereas Lisa's better suited to kicking a ball in the backyard with her dad.

"I'm glad you've time to pop in, there's something I need to tell you."

"Sounds ominous Mavis," I say putting Victor down. Mavis faffs about making the teas; she's prone to overthinking things and I can tell she's feeling uncomfortable. "Whatever it is Mavis, it can't be as bad as you've built it up to be." I'm tired and hope that this isn't going to be a taxing conversation.

She puts the tea tray down and says, "Well ..." then stalls for time, "I've some fruit shortcake in if you'd like one." I give her what I hope is a sympathetic smile and she continues, "I'm moving house –"

"That's a surprise," I interject, "somewhere nice?" Selfishly I hope it's not going to be too far away, the last thing I need is to find a new childminder, especially one as good as Mavis.

"I've not decided yet I'm also thinking about getting a little job ... a few hours a day, so it'll mean I can't have Victor."

"When are you moving?" I ask, while thinking, bloody hell, I will need to find a new childminder.

"Not sure yet, a month or so ..."

"Well, he's going to nursery in September, so he'll be there during the day and hopefully I'll be able to sort something for the few weeks before he starts at Summerbank Primary."

"Oh, there's no rush. I've not made up my mind up where I'll be going. I'm hoping it won't be too far so I can still pick the kiddies up after school for you."

I scold myself mentally for being so selfish, I know this can't be an easy decision for Mavis.

"That's fine Mavis, don't worry about it. What's brought on this change of situation?"

"Oh nothing really, you know getting older, wanting new things ..." She's not convincing me but I know not to push her for an answer, she'll tell me in time.

"Well, you've been a godsend these past years looking after Lisa and Victor," I say as my mind is sorting through possibilities for a new childminder for the few months Victor has left before nursery.

Mavis breathes out noisily, her relief obvious. "I was worried you'd be unhappy with me."

"Not at all, Just keep me informed and we'll work something out. Now I'd better get these horrors home for their tea. Will you be coming to Doreen's later for the unveiling of her new carpet?"

"I will. She's had the fitter in again today, said she wasn't happy with the way it looked and he's been back to relay the whole thing. Poor man's probably suffering from shell shock."

"Shell shock. You do know they've been calling it posttraumatic stress disorder for the past couple of years."

Mavis chuckles, "Well after being at Doreen's beck and call twice, he'll no doubt need to have a more scientifically named mental problem."

"Should we call for you later?"

"No need, I'll see you both there."

***

Doreen's house isn't like the mid-terraced properties Vera and I live in, Doreen's is the end house in a block of four, that she likes to call, her link detached. She purchased it under the Tory government's Right to Buy Scheme, using her late mother's life insurance. As soon as she was freehold rather than rental, she set about making it stand out from the others in the street. She's had the doors and windows replaced, the front garden paved and adorned with a concrete bird bath and other assorted mass-produced garden statuary and painted her front gate purple.

We close the gate behind us, walk up the path and ring her doorbell that plays the 'Russian Dance' from Tchaikovsky's, *Nutcracker*. Vera's tempted as usual to have a bash at some Cossack dancing and as she's mid squat Doreen opens the door and says, "Must you?"

"I can't help it, it's the doorbell, it sets off my inner Ukrainian."

"Come in Beryl," Doreen says, "I see your friend is as flippant as always." I stifle a laugh and push Vera in front of me. "Shoe's off!" Doreen says and hands us both a pair of slippers that she's obviously purchased in advance of her carpet reveal.

We're ushered through into her sitting room and greeted by the sight of a strange man's bum crack peeking over the waistband of his trousers.

"I had planned for the fitting to be completed by five but Royston here was late arriving." A man who looked harassed turned and looked over his shoulder at us before returning to fiddle with the carpet and a gripper bar.

Doreen moves into the kitchen and I follow her, leaving Vera asking the carpet fitter if he has to purchase trousers with reinforced knees for work.

"Shall I ask Royston if he'd like tea?"

"Heavens, no." Doreen replies, "he's had two already, and a slice of cake, another cup and he'll be here for another hour."

Just then, Royston enters the kitchen, pops his mug and plate on the counter and says he's finished. "I'll be getting off now. It's been nice … to err… know you."

"I'll see you out," Doreen ushers him into the hallway, and I hear her say, "Your work boots are in the plant pot outside the front door."

When Doreen returns I've made a pot of tea and washed up Royston's crockery and I'm just putting them away when she says, "That doesn't go in the cupboard, it's the dog's plate."

"But this is the plate you gave to the carpet fitter."

"That's right Beryl. He's a manual worker so I didn't trust him with my dinnerware."

"But it's…"

"Don't worry, I'm sure the dog won't mind."

We're whisked into the sitting room to admire the carpet with Doreen standing over us as we make our appreciative assessment of the orange and claret swirls. "Looks like a dropped pizza," Vera says, earning her a flinty look.

"Now," Doreen says, her plucked eyebrows relaxing as she indicates she'd like us to sit down. "I'm not one to censor speech, but when Mavis arrives I think we should avoid any conversational subjects that centre around marital disharmony … Adultery, relocation, last week's episode of *Dallas* and suchlike."

"Yes, Cliff Barnes and Sue Ellen are at it again," Vera pipes up.

"That's exactly the sort of thing we need to avoid in Mavis's presence."

"What are you getting at, Doreen," I ask, bemused by her cryptic clues.

"Very well, but you didn't hear it from me." Vera and I nod our heads conspiratorially. "Mavis's husband, Gerry has been having an affair with the woman out of the travel agents in Tower Square."

"Poor Mavis, is it serious?" I ask.

"I should think so, they've run away together."

Just then the 'Russian Dance' doorbell sings again and Doreen stands saying, remember no mention of D.I.V.O.R.C.E."

"Bloody hell, who does she think she is …" Vera says, "Tammy Wynette?"

Mavis comes into the room sporting her requisite slippers and I'm looking across at the others; Doreen is chewing the inside of her cheek with worry while Vera sits with a devilish grin and I hope my face remains neutral. There's a few minutes of carpet-related chat, where Vera once again mentions that the pattern looks like a dropped pizza and we settle down to enjoy a fresh pot of tea when Vera blurts out, "So, I hear your fella's run off with that flighty piece out of the travel agents." Doreen chokes on a mouthful of tea and Mavis just nods.

"Where've they gone, somewhere exotic, Thailand ... Ibiza?"

"Llandudno."

"Llandudno. Are you telling me your husband's been getting his leg over with an international travel agent and the furthest they can relocate to is North Wales? If that's the case, you're better off without him."

Mavis's shoulders shudder, she sniffs and we're all poised for the waterworks but they don't come, she lets out a shriek and starts laughing like her life depends on it, and between breaths, she says, "You can always guarantee Vera will make a situation seem less of a calamity and more like a comedy."

I join in with the laughter as does Vera, meanwhile, Doreen sits stony-faced, I'm guessing because no one is paying attention to her newly laid carpet.

2. Toasties

Thursday 15 April 1982
Well, what a month April has been so far. At work, we started the month with the usual pranks for April Fools' Day. Patricia had screamed when someone hid a plastic spider beneath her sponges and poor Ricky was sent to packing for a 'long weight,' – the play on words never failing to amuse the older chaps in the clay end.

I worked an hour extra each day in the run-up to Easter to increase my piecework counts. I needed those few extra pounds in my wage packet to pay for Easter eggs for Lisa and Victor, and even a small one for Len. I knew he wouldn't bother buying any; not that he doesn't care, it's a man-thing isn't it? However, I did laugh the other evening, our Lisa, had been making an Easter bonnet in school and asked her father if he would be making himself one. "Men dunna wear bonnets, my lovely" he'd replied to her question.

"Why not?"
"Because they're blokes."
"Why should that stop them?"
"Because that's the way things are."
"But why?"
"Go and ask your mother," was his final word on the subject. He got up from his chair and escaped into the backyard, where he put the dog on its lead and took it for an impromptu walk.

The most disturbing thing to have happened this month was the announcement that we are at war with Argentina. Apparently, it's over some islands that most of the British population didn't seem to know existed. Normally, news reports like this make me shake my head and wonder what the world is coming to, but this time, the news really hit home.

On the 2nd of the month, Vera arrived at work in a bit of a tizzy, she wasn't able to focus and burst into tears while eating a bacon and cheese oatcake. "I'm worried Emmett will be posted to these Falkland Islands," she said.

"Emmett's your husband, isn't he?" Donna asked.

"Yes, he's in the Royal Navy."

"So will he be sailing into a warzone?" Patricia asked, subtlety not being her strong suit.

"We don't know," I stepped in, then turning to Vera I said, "I'm sure he'll be okay, I think this whole war is just a storm in a teacup."

"I hope so," Vera said, sniffing.

"What's the worst that can happen?" Patricia said and everyone looked at her incredulously.

"Apart from him getting killed, the cost of tinned corned beef could rocket," and Vera took a bite of her oatcake.

***

Kathleen's engagement invitations stated that the party was being hosted in the function suite at the Potter's Wheel pub. The function suite turns out to be a room above the public lounge. It features a glittered curtain on one wall and a small bar shoved into a corner next to the lavatories. The disco is already set up under the tinsel curtain and we are welcomed by Phil Oakey singing, 'Don't You Want Me.' I smile, thinking, with Kathleen's romantic track record this could be seen as foreshadowing the success of her latest union. We've already got drinks from the bar downstairs and spotting a free table we lay claim to it, draping coats over stools and shoving our handbags under the gold, cast iron legs. Tony, the DJ, a man with his shirt open to his navel, displaying enough chest hair to stuff a sofa waves to us, "Hello girls, are you all ready for a good time?" he says over the microphone as he grabs his crotch and thrusts his hips forward.

"What's wrong, you got crabs?" Donna shouts back.

Followed by Stella who says, "I've some lotion in me bag for them."

Tony's leer crumbles and turning away, the Human League is replaced by the J Geils Band.

"I've put your present on the table with mine," Vera says joining us.

"What did you get?" Stella asks.

"A Breville toastie maker."

"That's quite extravagant Vera."

"Not really, it was an unwanted Christmas present."

"It's not the one you won in the work's raffle is it?"

Vera thinks for a while and then says, "It could be. Oh well, I've never used it so waste not want not."

The music is interrupted by a fanfare and Kathleen and her new fiancé, a lanky lad named Nigel enter the room. Kathleen's dyed her hair orange and styled it to look like Toyah and Nigel is wearing silver trousers, lip gloss and eyeliner. He looks uncomfortable, self-consciously looking down at his shoes and displaying white splashes in his hair.

"I see he's come as a second-rate Adam Ant," Patricia says.

"Adam Ant, more like Sidney stick insect," laughs Stella.

"What does she see in him?" Vera says. "I've seen more meat on a sparrow's leg."

"He's probably a very nice young man … "I add.

"He'd have to be," Stella interrupts, "He was obviously in the bum queue when God was giving out faces."

"Hello girls, have you seen my ring?" Kathleen says, and I squeeze Vera's hand to stop her from coming out with a less-than-polite reply. "This is my fiancé Nigel. He's a painter and decorator."

"That explains the splashes in his hair," Patricia says.

"Thank goodness, I was wondering if he had a pigeon loft at home," Vera adds.

"Yes, he's so tall his head almost touches the ceilings in the houses where he works." Kathleen points out giving Nigel an encouraging smile.

"Yeah, low ceilings are a bother," he mumbles.

"Do you know what you need lad?" Vera says smiling. "A haircut like our Donna," she points across the room to her Mohican haircut, "then you'd be able to paint the ceilings and the walls at the same time." Nigel's response is a weak smile before Kathleen whisks him away.

A cheer goes up as Tony the DJ puts 'Come on Eileen' on the turntable and a tsunami of bodies in flouncy blouses and oversized belts invade the dancefloor. With everyone gyrating the cloying smell of Dior's Poison permeates the air. Off-key voices too-ra-loo-rye-ay along with Dexys and hairstyles set with enough hairspray to glue together a biplane's wings start to wilt. The record ends and walking back to the table we spot Hilary from packing, waddling towards us in what looks like sprayed-on denim.

"Hi Hilary," Stella says. "are those the Bananarama inspired baggy jeans you got from the catalogue?

"Yes, but I think they've sent the wrong size."

"You should have sent them back."

"I will after tonight, my cousin Shaz works in Top Shop. She's said she'll take them into work and attach the labels back on for me, so they don't look worn."

"But what if they smell?" says Stella.

"No chance of that, I'm wearing two pairs of knickers and I'll give them a quick going over with some Shake n Vac."

The conversation is interrupted by gate crashers: Doreen and Mavis join us despite not having an invite. "We heard there was a do upstairs and thought we'd see who was here," Mavis says. "Oh you look nice Hilary; skintight jeans really suit you." Hilary's eyes widen and she makes her excuses and walks away.

"I thought she was on a diet," Doreen says as Mavis goes to the bar to fetch drinks.

"She's on a sensible eating regime," I tell her.

"Yes, a more balanced diet," Stella adds.

Hilary's idea of a balanced diet," Vera interjects, "is having a bacon sandwich in both hands."

Mavis returns with a round of drinks for everyone at our table saying, "I'm spending Gerry's money, he'll wet himself when he gets his credit card bill. Cheers everyone." Laughter follows and Tony announces that the buffet is open and people fall upon it like a wake of ravenous vultures. Vera gets up and I see her push her way through the throng and reemerge with a large plate piled high with sandwiches and sausage rolls. "Here we go, I've got enough for all of us," she says putting the plate down. "I tried to get some quiche but before I could grab any, a spotty lad in the queue coughed on it, so I thought it was best left alone."

I reach across for an egg and cress sandwich when Stella leans in and asks, "Have you mentioned the holiday idea to your Len yet?"

"Not yet, I thought I'd bring it up at the weekend, he'll be more responsive after a pale ale in his own chair."

"Men, they're so predictable," she says, and I agree.

We're all having a pleasant time and the music's encouraging people to dance. Mavis has bought another round of drinks, followed by glasses of something the colour of urine, which she tells us is Pernod and lemonade. The floor around the buffet table is a mess of trodden in pastry and dropped ham baps. The party seems to be going as planned when suddenly there's a commotion from across the room. Conversations hush and we all turn to see Kathleen – her hair colour has run and she now looks like a furious carrot – shouting at Nigel, who looks a little dishevelled and has a smear of red across his mouth.

"Ooh, it's all kicking off over there," Donna says arriving at the table holding hands with Ricky. "Kathleen went into the loos and found Nigel snogging with another girl. She points to someone who looks remarkably like Kim Wilde."

"Nigel said he got dazzled by the disco lights …"

"In the toilets?" I ask.

"Kathleen doesn't believe him; she's called off the engagement …"

"… so, we're off to Chico's."

"… the music's much better …"

"… not so many oldies either." Donna and Ricky say, the youngsters finishing off each other's sentences.

"Well, that's a turn-up for the books," I say to the others as we watch them slip away for a night of alternative music in the Hanley nightclub.

The music stops just as Kathleen and the Kim lookalike begin pulling at each other's hair and swearing. Nigel is looking on, his mascara smudged under his eyes making him resemble a self-conscious panda. The lights go on and the landlord tells everyone to leave, a chorus of groans erupts and people gather up their belongings and trudge downstairs.

"Come on, get these down you," Mavis says pointing to the yellow drinks. We all swallow the aniseed beverage in one gulp before making our way out of the function room bypassing the gifts table, so that Vera can take back her Breville to recycle somewhere else.

***

Saturday mornings are usually taken up with the family shop, but today I've arrived at Vera's with a couple of apple turnovers; at least the inevitable pastry detritus will fall onto her own carpet today. I love my friend but she's got no control over what she eats. Sauces end up down her top, chocolate around her mouth and pastry is spread far and wide like an eczema sufferer in front of a desk fan.

During our tea and turnovers, we discussed the debacle that had been Kathleen's engagement. Apparently, Nigel went home with the other girl and Kathleen ended up being consoled by Tony the DJ, who we both admit, gave us the creeps. Donna has been circumspect about her night out with Ricky, however, the love bite on his neck on Friday morning was telling.

"How are you feeling?" I ask her.

"About Emmett?"

"Yes, of course about Emmett, it can't be easy not knowing if he's on his way to war."

"I knew when I married him this was a possibility, but as you said, I'm hoping it will blow over pretty quickly."

"Thatcher seems determined to fight it out."

"Yes, I saw her on the news. I hope she doesn't just use this as an excuse to salve her reputation. There's lives at stake."

"I'm sure the people in charge will make the right decisions."

"Yes, because don't they always Beryl."

Vera's response is tinged with sarcasm and I can see she's not really up for talking about Emmett's possible dilemma. I change the subject to Mavis and the liberal use of her feckless husband's credit card. "She went out yesterday and treated herself to a foot spa and pair of hair crimpers."

"Crimpers, with her hair she'll look like she's got a Cornish pasty and her head."

"At least her feet will be fragrant."

We go into town together to get our shopping and I can see that Vera's preoccupied, at one point she's putting cat food in her trolley, which I have to remove as she doesn't have a cat. When we get to the checkout she's asking where the tin of tuna she took off the shelves has gone. "I bet someone nicked it out of my trolley when my back was turned."

"Would you like me to ask someone to fetch you some?" the girl at the checkout asks her.

"No it's all right love, I've some tinned ham in at home."

The checkout girl looks at me and I shrug, it's always been a difficult task fathoming out the inner workings of Vera's mind.

We've been friends for years, bridesmaids at each other's weddings and she and Emmett are godparents to my children. Vera's not been blessed with children, she has according to Mavis, 'deceptive' ovaries. At first, she was upset about the prospect of being childless, but as time moved on she accepted it. Sometimes she may joke about the joy of not having Marmite handprints on her wallpaper or treading on rogue pieces of Lego, but I think she feels she's somehow missed out. Throughout the best of times and the worst of times – that sounds strangely familiar – we've been there for each other, and I'll be here for her during this time of uncertainty until Emmett is back home and we're all sitting in the working men's club with drinks and a game of bingo.

Back from shopping, we're in Vera's kitchen where she's taken the Breville from its box and put all the packaging aside so she can repack it to give as a gift at a later date. She's putting slices of buttered white bread inside and says, "I'm making Bernard a ham and cheese toastie."

I watch as she peels a thin slice of ham away from the pack and drapes it across a hunk of cheddar, then say, "I thought he was moving out?"

"He's going into sheltered housing in a week. His daughter's glad the council found him a space."

"Will you miss looking after him?" Vera pauses to think. She's been looking after her elderly neighbour, Bernard for over a year, ever since he lost his temper and threw a bowl of cream of chicken soup at his home help. "I don't think so," Vera says. "He's becoming more belligerent as time goes by. Honestly, he'd complain if his arse was on fire and he needed a light for his fag." She removes the hot toastie from the Breville and sets it down to cool. "I'll take this 'round in a minute, the last thing he needs is molten cheese, with his loose dentures the cheddar might fuse them permanently to his gums." She then peels a banana and says, "According to the recipe book enclosed, the Breville makes sweet toasties too. Pass me that Bounty and I'll make us both a 'nana and coconut chocolate one."

I'm dreading the result of this concoction but carry on, "Are you still doing his washing?"

"Goodness no! I stopped doing that a while ago, it's his daughter's responsibility now. I refuse to be besieged by dirty underpants that display what he's eaten the day before."

"Do you know who'll be moving in when he's gone?"

"Yes, a lovely family. I met them last week. Mrs Khan and her son."

***

Len's in the middle room, sitting in his chair opposite the television as I make his tea, he's watching the *Dukes of Hazzard;* he claims it's because he likes the storylines but I suspect he's more than likely transfixed by Daisy Duke in her hotpants.

Lisa's at the table colouring in while Victor watches her. I carry Len's tea into him on a tray. "This is a bit early isn't it," he says.

"I thought we could get it over and done with and it'll give us chance to have a talk after I've bathed the kids before you go to the club."

"Talk about what? ... Is there any HP sauce?"

"It's coming," I call from the kitchen.

Len hits the bottom of the bottle with his palm, dolloping gobs of the brown sauce onto his bacon chop and mash.

"Oh mum, it's early yet, I don't want a bath, I want to watch telly," Lisa complains.

"You can watch some telly once you're in your nightie," I tell her as I march the children out of the room and upstairs.

I'm elbow-deep in Matey bubbles wondering what Len's reaction to the holiday idea will be. It's not that he's the type of husband to stop a wife from having her own interests, in fact, he encourages me to be as independent as I want to be and says he'd hate for me to be one of those wives who're dependent on their husbands and can't seem to think for themselves. He likes to pride himself on being, as he calls it, a progressive husband, even if he's incapable of making his own meals.

Victor looks angelic in his striped pyjamas sitting in my chair beside the fire while Lisa, despite having had her hair shampooed and brushed, still manages to look like she's spent an hour with a whirling dervish. Len's taken his dishes into the kitchen, washed and put them away, and made a pot of tea in my absence. I'm lowering myself onto the sofa when he asks what I want to talk about.

"Well, some of the girls at work are thinking it might be nice if we all went away for a little holiday, a sort of girl's trip. But if you're –"

"When?" he interrupts.

"Start of the potters' holidays."

"First Monday until Wednesday?"

"Yes, just … hang on, how do you know what dates they're talking about?" Len chuckles, "You already know don't you?"

"Of course. There are no secrets on a potbank. Stella's already asked her fella."

"And what's he said?"

"Who cares what he's said, it's what I say that matters isn't it?" Len does his best to sound authoritative but forgets I know him too well. I smile and wait and he says, "It's up to you love, if you fancy a break with the girls that's fine by me, I can cope with the little ones for two nights on one condition."

"What, no dancing with strange men?"

"I'm not bothered about who you dance with … just as long as it's only jigging on the dance floor, but please promise me you won't ask Mavis or Doreen to look in on us while you're away."

"I promise." I lean in and kiss the top of his head.

"Oh, and duck … no dancing with strange men."

3. Emergency Milk

Tuesday 4 May 1982
Len had just got up to turn off the television when a BBC news report came on. John Humphreys told the nation that an Exocet missile had hit the HMS Sheffield resulting in a loss of life. The news continued as we both stood in silence in our middle room, me holding two cooling cups of cocoa. Dialogue from the report drifted out from the screen: 'The prime minister was informed at 6 pm,' 'The first loss of a ship in 37 years.' Then a list of telephone numbers was displayed for the next of kin to contact, for information about the ship's crew.

"Vera," Len said.

One word.

Only one word was needed and he turned the television off.

***

The factory is buzzing with last night's news, people from different parts of the potbank – ghouls, Stella has called them – have wandered into the biscuit department to gaze at Vera's empty bench. People know we're close and questions are being asked of me. People I've never spoken to before are eager for news, for gossip, for anything that will give them a titbit to dangle temptingly before their own friendship groups.

Andrew has just told two women from another department to get back to their benches rather than disturb his 'girls.'

"Beryl," he calls and I go over to his office which is just four plasterboard walls with windows that butt up against a desk. It's barely big enough for two people to fit inside but he manages to close the door behind me and offers me his seat.

"I'm not being nosey, just wondering, have you spoken with Vera?"

I shake my head, I'm sick of talking about it this morning.

"She hasn't called in to say she'll be absent … Which is understandable," he adds quickly. "If you want to go to her, I'll sign you out and you'll still get paid for today."

I look up at the man in the round, owl-like glasses and tell him, "I'm not bothered about the money. But I would like to go to her."

"I understand. Now you get yourself off, I'll sign your clock card."

"I'll make up my counts over the next few days," I tell him.

"Honestly, Beryl, there's no need. Do what you have to do."

I'm starting to rinse out my sponges when Stella looks over, "Are you off to see Vera?"

"Yes."

"Leave that, I'll clean your bench down for you. Let Vee, know we're all thinking of her."

I thank her and promise to pass on her thoughts and picking up my bag I leave.

I'm walking up the same road I walk along every day, but somehow today it feels longer. It feels like each step is an effort. On the way I pass the doctor's surgery and a woman asks if I've heard anything about Vera's husband. I'm not normally rude but I don't answer her, I look straight ahead and carry on walking, if I stop, I know I will start to cry.

Outside the front door, I stand for a few seconds, pausing before I knock. I'm not sure why, nervous trepidation probably. I knock and a crack appears, growing slowly wider until Vera's eyes are showing. I hear her mutter, "It's you," before the door opens fully to reveal her wrapped in a dressing gown. "Shouldn't you be at work?"

"Sometimes there are more important things than putting handles on cups." I step inside and follow her up the hallway into the middle room.

"Tea?" she says.

One word, again.

"I'll do it," I tell her.

"No, I can manage, sit down."

I'm sitting in a chair listening to her rattling around her kitchen, usually, she'd be chattering away so it's odd to have no conversation just the sound of spoons on china. I look around the room. I've seen it so many times, I could tell you with my eyes closed where every knick-knack is, what every picture depicts and how many coasters there are on her coffee table. But today it feels different, like something is missing. Like a die minus its spots, familiar but lacking.

"I've only got emergency milk," Vera says popping her head around the door jamb.

"That'll be fine," I tell her.

Emergency milk is UHT in a carton that Vera keeps for an emergency should she run out of fresh milk, which to my knowledge, is something she's never done before.

She carries in the tray and puts it down on the coffee table in front of the sofa and asks if I can pour the cups. I pick up the carton of milk and notice it's several months out of date. I'm going to open it regardless but she asks, "What's wrong?"

"Nothing," I say.

Vera takes the carton reads the date and walks back into the kitchen, I hear the drawer open and go to look and see her cutting a corner from the carton and tipping the milk down the sink. "I might have some powdered," she says.

"I'll go to the shop and fetch some fresh," I tell her and she walks back into the middle room and puts a cosy over the teapot.

When I return, she's changed out of her nightwear. "I didn't go to bed last night," she says, standing in the middle of the room as I pour the tea that's now stewed.

"I would have phoned but ..."

"I know."

We're silent. Vera stays standing and I sit, hugging my lukewarm tea. The clock on the chimney breast is loud, tick, tick, tick, counting away the seconds that hang in the air like phantoms waiting to fall around us. I stand and move into the kitchen to make a fresh pot of tea and when I return Vera still hasn't moved. I place a fresh cup of tea down for her and she looks down at it and then up at the clock. "I've phoned his base, but there's no news yet."

"Well, what is it they say?"

"No news is good news ... that's bollocks, Beryl. No news just delays the bad news."

"You can't be sure."

"I am ... I know ... Here." She punches herself above her heart. "I know." Suddenly she becomes animated, "I haven't offered you a biscuit. You'd never be so inhospitable. Let me fetch some."

"No. Vera!" I raise my voice and she stops midway to the kitchen. "Leave the bloody biscuits and come and sit down."

She does as she's asked and then looking directly at me she says, "I haven't cried. Not a single tear. I can't, not until I know. I know, I said I know, but I don't know really, do I? It's the not knowing that's ..." her words peter out, and she picks up her drink and takes a sip.

I stay with her all day. Fix her something to eat and engage in the brief sporadic moments of conversation she allows past her lips. She refuses to have the TV or radio on and when some mail arrives she rushes to collect it from the hallway as if it will be bringing her the news she seeks.

Later that day the news arrives in a telephone call. I hear her side of the conversation, it's made up of her confirming her name, followed by monotone replies of, 'yes', 'no' and 'I see.' She puts the phone down and then she cries.

***

Today, I've answered a few questions, but kept my own counsel regarding Vera's situation and the majority of the chatter on the line was the proposed 'girls' holiday idea. How quickly themes change.

"So, what did Len say?" Stella asked me at the sinks earlier.

"He said it's up to me," I told her.

"So are you going to come? It's only eight weeks off."

"I don't think Vera will be up for it so soon, and I'd like to stay and make sure she's okay."

A part of me wants to have a break with the others from work, but there's no instruction manual about how to deal with losing a loved one who's on the other side of the world. So I think I'd rather stay here and keep an eye on my best friend. I know it's what she'd do if our roles were reversed.

***

Len's made tea tonight, when I say made tea, he's fetched fish and chips from the chippy on Summerbank Road and opened a tin of mushy peas and warmed them in the microwave. There are five places laid at the table, I'm about to ask him why when there's a knock at the front door. "I'll go," Lisa shouts.

"No you will not, young lady," Len shouts and he marches down the hall as usual to grab her by the hand.

I look up as Vera comes into the middle room, "Thanks for the invite to tea," she says.

Catching up, I say, "That's okay ... cuppa?"

"No," Len says and disappears into the kitchen, to return holding a bottle of Lambrusco aloft. He puts it on the table and exits to dish up.

We adults eat in companionable silence, Victor pushes his peas around the plate pulling a face while Lisa gabbles on about her day at school and when all the knives and forks are put down she says, "I'm going on a trip with school."

"Really, where?" says Vera and Lisa gets down from the table and fetches a crumpled sheet of paper and hands it to her.

"It's about a trip to some caves."

Vera reads and then says, "I've been here. Treak Cliff Cavern. You'll like it, they have stalactites that hang down like dragon's teeth."

"Dragons. I want to see," Victor says.

"You can't go 'cause you're too little."

"But I ..." Victor's lip juts out and before he can get too upset Len steps in.

"Button it, Lisa, otherwise you won't be going either."

"Did you go by yourself?" she asks, undeterred by her father.

"No," Vera says handing back the letter, "I went with Uncle Emmett."

"That's enough Lisa," I say, but Vera reaches over and places her hand on top of mine to indicate it's okay.

"Uncle Emmett bought me some Blue John from a nearby gift shop, I'll show you next time you come round. It's in my jewellery box."

"Who is Blue John?" Lisa asks.

"Blue John's not a person, it's a purple-coloured stone from a cave near where you're going to visit," Vera tells her.

"So why isn't it called Purple John?"

"I don't know," and Vera laughs, "perhaps it should be."

Len offers to get the children ready for bed and after the table's cleared Vera and I sit by the hearth, each with a glass of Lambrusco in our hands. We talk about the factory, and I tell her that everyone is sending their condolences.

"Are you going on the holiday that's being arranged?" She's swerving the subject, who can blame her?

"No. Len said, he didn't mind looking after the kids if I wanted to go, but I've told Stella I'll be giving it a miss."

"I hope you didn't turn down the chance because of me."

"No," I lie, "I just didn't fancy it."

"My sister has asked if I'd like to go to stay for a while," Vera says. "I thanked her but said I'd rather stay at home."

"Maybe she could come and stay with you, would you like that?"

"Goodness, no. And put up with her Irish music obsession."

"Is she still listening to the Dubliners every day?"

"Isn't she just. Do you know something, Beryl? I don't know where her fascination with Irish music comes from, we don't have a family history from there, and to be quite frank if she plays me another fiddle and tin whistle combination, I'll be serving time at Her Majesty's pleasure. Anyway, how's *your* sister?"

"You know, okay I guess."

"Family, eh? We can't pick them can we, we just have to swallow hard and say nowt."

"I was thinking of taking the kids to the park on Saturday when you two go for dinner at Mavis's," Len says coming back into the room. "Kids are in bed, Victor's fast asleep and Lisa's reading one of her, '*Worst Witch'* books.

"Thanks, duck," I say, "It's nice of Mavis to invite us round, don't you think?"

"Gives us a chance to find out more about Gerry's indiscretion," Vera replies.

"Takes the emphasis off your troubles too."

"That's so true, Len, gets me off the hook so to speak."

Len walks Vera home and I wash up the dinner dishes before settling back into my chair with a cup of tea and the book I've borrowed from the library. Usually, I like these moments of peace when the children are in bed and there's nothing to do but read, however, tonight I'm at odds with myself. I can't settle. Maybe it's because I'm wrapped up in Vera's grief and it's making me think about life and how quickly it can change. Thoughts float around my head like butterflies over a meadow, I think about Vera's comments about her sister and I begin to wonder how mine is. We haven't spoken for a long time. It's not unusual, for these periods of non-communication, it's just how we are. How we've become.

We're very different people, she likes order, everything in its place. Unlike me, she's unmarried despite being a couple of years older. She says it's because she's career minded but I have my suspicion it's really because she's not inclined to become part of a couple. I'll give her a call maybe tomorrow, just to check how she is. I know she'll rabbit on about something that will give her an air of superiority and I'll come away feeling deflated, like a sponge cake when the oven door's been opened too soon. I do worry about her living alone, in much the same way as I do for Doreen. I guess not everyone is like me. I'm happy having another person to share everything with. To be one of a pair, like gloves or socks. Len is my other glove, he's a perfect fit. What I mean by perfect isn't that he's the best at most things, or he's flawless. He's a bit rough around the edges, well not so much rough as frayed and he's not gregarious. He knows what he likes and tends to stick with it, and I'm grateful it's me he likes. He's a good husband, he provides well for us, and he's liberal in so much as he's open to change.

I hear the back door open and Len calls to say he's home and asks me to get the corkscrew out of the drinks cabinet. "I called into the off licence on the way back from Vera's and grabbed a bottle of wine for us, thought you'd like a drop."

"What's this, Len Bickerstaff drinking wine instead of brown ale, people will talk."

"Let 'em," he says and pours two glasses of red and passes one to me. "I hope you didn't mind me asking Vera round for tea?"

"No, it was a very kind thing to do." I lean across and kiss him. "I'm proper lucky to have you."

"I know," he says, then pulls a packet of pork scratchings from his jacket pocket and says, "D'you want one?"

4. Blackpool

Sunday 27 June 1982
I've just nipped to Vera's to confirm the coach times for tomorrow. I knocked at the front door but there was no reply so I walked up the backsies and found her standing at next door's back gate. "Oh, hello Beryl," she says seeing me, "this is my new neighbour, Mrs Khan."

"Pleased to meet you," I say to the small Indian woman in a traditional sari. "Are you settling in?"

"Yes, thank you," she replies and shuffles back inside her house.

"She's quite shy," Vera says ushering me up her yard and into her kitchen. Putting the kettle on she adds, "I think, it's because she struggles with the English language."

We take our cups of tea into Vera's middle room and sitting down she says, "I've loaned her a book to help with her English."

"I hope it wasn't one of these," I pick up a Jackie Collins from the coffee table.

"No, I thought I'd keep it simple, so she doesn't learn words she won't need to use."

"American ones, such as sidewalk or elevator."

"I was thinking more of orgasm or fellatio."

I sip my tea and say no more and after a few minutes of silence I say, "Are you ready for tomorrow?"

"I think so. Do you think I'll need to pack a hairdryer?"

"I was wondering the same thing."

"You pack yours then, and we can share it. Fancy a wagon wheel?"

Here we go I think as Vera unwraps hers and starts to nibble around the edge like a beaver on a roundabout, turning the chocolate wheel as it decreases in size as she eats it. I fight the urge to say something about yet another of her idiosyncratic ways of eating and just take a bite from mine.

***

A few days ago while we were having coffee and cake at Doreen's, Vera let slip that there was a 'girls' trip at work and I'd decided not to tag along.

"I'd love a mini break," Mavis had said, "What about you lot?"

I said nothing, not wanting to put Vera in an uncomfortable situation when she blurted out, "I'd have liked a break too. Now I'm back at work I've got to start just getting on with things, there's nothing I can do really. Not until I've heard from the Navy."

"Well!" Doreen had said and walked into her hall to make a telephone call, and coming back said, "That's it, it's sorted. We're off to Blackpool for two nights."

So this morning we boarded a coach at Hanley and the four of us made our way north. We arrive at Fairview, a guest house owned by Doreen's cousin, and we're standing in reception checking in with Wilma, a tall woman with copper-coloured hair, blue mascara and bosoms you could balance a tray on.

"Right, she says," licking a finger topped with an orange-painted nail before flicking through a ledger. "I wouldn't have the space to accommodate you if my regulars from Spalding hadn't had a family emergency concerning a vacuum cleaner and a pot of Vaseline. I have since secured another booking but they won't arrive until Wednesday, so you can have two nights, sharing, with breakfast. I don't do evening meals and although there's a kettle in the rooms, can I ask that you don't make yourselves mugs of instant soup, the smell tends to hang about in the soft furnishings."

Wilma hands us our keys, tells us the room numbers and then once again, for effect, reminds us that because it's last minute and she's related to Doreen the price is discounted heavily.

Our room is adequate, with twin beds and a shared bathroom down the landing. Vera's inspecting the inside of the kettle and counting how many tea bags we've been allocated and says, "She was a bit fierce wasn't she?"

"Wilma ... Yes she's quite formidable."

"Formidable, she'd make a hard-nosed prison officer look like a nursery nurse."

The bathroom's clean," I say; I've already taken a walk down the landing. Vera crosses the room and looks out of the window and I ask her what the view's like.

She starts laughing, "What's this place called? Fairview?" She beckons me over and pulls back the curtain, "There's a view that's far from fair." And I look across at the hotel opposite to see a naked man of advancing years bending over. "He'll need some decent underpants to stop those banging against his knees."

"I can't unsee it," I say laughing just as he stands up and turns around and spots us. He cups himself and Vera gives him a wave before he pulls the curtains shut.

"I never knew everything dropped as men got older."

"You've got that to look forward to with your Len," she says and I catch a shadow cross her eyes as she realises. Quickly I change the mood by filling the kettle, rinsing the mugs out and dropping in two tea bags.

We sit on the beds drinking tea after we've commandeered a drawer each and unpacked the few things we've brought with us. Vera's hung her 'going out' dress on the outside of the wardrobe ready for tonight and my outfit's draped over a chair.

"What do you think of the wallpaper?" Vera says.

"It's horrible, looks like it was put up by a decorator with astigmatism."

"It clashes with the bed covers."

"And the lampshade," I add.

"We'll have to make sure we don't get too drunk tonight otherwise when we come back we'll think we're having a 1970's psychedelic experience."

The knock at our door curtails our laughter and Mavis pops her head in. "Wilma tells me there's a nice place a few streets away that does a nice chicken in a basket, or scampi if that's what we'd prefer."

"Scampi in a basket, have we stepped back in time?" Vera says.

"Yes, the 1970's," I reply and Mavis looks confused as the two of us start laughing again.

The evening is quite pleasant, there's a gentle breeze off the sea and the remnants of the late June day mean it's not cold. We're out without jackets, although Doreen's insisted we all bring a cardigan each. "Without warning, the weather here can be quite cutting," she tells us. It's early and so the beachfront is populated by parents marching children with sand-covered knees back to boarding houses, while groups of friends, like us, are off out for their evening meal.

"I fancy fish and chips. You can't come to the seaside and not have fish and chips," Mavis says.

"I fancy something different for a change," pipes up Vera.

"Such as?" I ask.

"I don't know, something exotic."

"Like salmonella?" Doreen adds her two-penn'orth to the conversation and steers us away from a man selling burgers and hot dogs from a van.

We gravitate to the tower, there's something about the attraction that draws visitors to it, it's our mini Eiffel, a place for ballroom dancing and afternoon tea. We're walking past Coral Island amusement arcade and despite protests, Mavis drags us all inside and we spend an hour feeding pennies into machines that push, buzz and shriek. Vera's having a whale of a time with a push-penny machine, trying her best to win the pile on the edge that's filled with riding coins and the occasional key ring or other piece of plastic nonsense. "I love these machines," she says, "I could sit and watch people play this all day. They should make a TV show."

"Don't be daft," I tell her, "who'd watch that."

"I'm really enjoying myself," Mavis says waving a paper bucket of coins, she's been lucky on the one-armed bandits. Doreen has succumbed to peer pressure and spent a few pence on a machine, but as she didn't win she put her purse away. After a few more goes on the bandits Mavis tips her winnings into her handbag and we leave the amusements laughing loudly. I have my arm around Vera's shoulders and anyone looking on would see a group of women in their mid-thirties acting like twenty-year-olds.

We take a walk through the streets behind the tower and wander past the Houndshill shopping centre, it's closing for the evening but we all agree that Hanley would benefit from a modern centre filled with shops. "We'll have to write to the council when we get home," I say just as Vera points to a sign advertising a Greek restaurant.

"What sort of food do you think *they* serve?" Mavis asks.

"Greek food," Doreen says, stating the obvious.

"No, I mean will it be nice?" She looks at the menu posted in the window, "They do moussaka. I remember Gerry telling me he'd tried it."

"Was that with his travel agent girlfriend?"

"I don't know … and do you know what … I don't care, even if they ate their way around the world on their secret dates."

"Just imagine it," I say, "Greek, Chinese, Italian, Indian. All those different kinds of food."

"No wonder I was spending more money than usual on toilet air fresheners."

"Mavis, must you?" Doreen says outraged.

Mavis laughs and asks, "What's a stifado?"

"Something your Gerry's entertaining his girlfriend with."

"That's put me right off," Mavis says pulling a face and we move on down the street towards the seafront with Doreen tutting loudly.

The aroma of fresh doughnuts pulls us around the corner and towards a stall where a jolly-looking man is serving. "Hello ladies," he says, "What can I get for you?"

"Four please," Mavis says, then turning around she tells us she's paying and we wait with blistering hot balls of sugary dough in paper bags as she counts out a multitude of pennies from her winnings. We find a bench overlooking the sand and sit down attempting Vera's suggestion that we take bites but not lick our lips – surprisingly Doreen wins the game and puts it down to not wearing lipstick like the rest of us.

The evening crowds are now gathering, groups of women set off to play bingo and young men head to the bars. It's still early so the stags and hens haven't arrived yet and Doreen says we should find somewhere to eat before depravity hits the Golden Mile.

"Let's go back to that Greek place," Mavis says, "But no more jokes about erections."

"What about tzatziki sauce," Doreen suggests and we all stop walking and look at her. The shock must be evident on our faces as she says, "What?" and laughs.

The food was excellent, Vera and I had some sort of a kebab, skewered meat served with flatbread and salad, Doreen had a spanakopita, which turned out to be a pie in very flaky pastry and I was glad that Vera hadn't chosen it, otherwise, there'd be a trail of filo all the way back to Wilma's Fairview. Mavis had the stew and as we left the restaurant she said it was the most satisfying stiffy she'd ever had.

I wake early to gentle snoring coming from Vera's side of the room. I look across, she has her mouth open and one arm is hanging out of the covers. I take this moment to think about how happy I am. I have the life I've always wanted, a good job, a loving husband and great friendships. Should I feel embarrassed by this feeling, knowing that what's waiting back home for my best friend who's still asleep isn't so bright?

I can't begin to imagine how she's feeling, to have lost Emmett at such a young age, only 38 years old – does it make a difference how old a spouse is and how many years you've shared? – I guess I'll never know until it happens to me. Men usually pass first, but you never know, life can deal you many different hands and I guess it's all down to what card game you play. There's only one certainty with life, and that's its end.

I pull back the covers and drop two teabags into mugs, the hum of the kettle rouses Vera and she wakes up and stretches. "I had a great night's sleep," she says.

"Must have been the three vodka and limes you had."

"Me … vodka … I don't generally touch the stuff."

"Not when you're sober," I say as the kettle clicks off.

Suitably woken by the tea, the smell of frying bacon invites us downstairs for breakfast. The dining room has a window that looks out over the rear yard, reminding me of being at home and I briefly think about Len, he'll be giving the children their cereal now.

Mavis and Doreen are already waiting for us, sitting at a table beneath a large picture of a swan, its wings open and a naked couple standing inside looking across at each other. Nodding towards it Vera whispers, "I hope the sausages aren't that small." I nudge her as Wilma walks through a multi-coloured fly screen, she's carrying two glass jugs of juice. After placing them down she wipes her hands on her apron.

"I hope you all slept well. Help yourselves to cereal, there's Corn Flakes and Rice Krispies. I'll bring the toast through in a moment, I just need to know what you'd like with your Full English, beans or tomatoes."

"Beans *or* tomatoes?" Vera says.

"That's right, one or the other. And I know some folks can be iffy with black pudding, but you lot being from Stoke I guess you'll all want some on your plates," I see Mavis open her mouth to speak but Wilma carries on regardless, "I've middle bacon, smoked because that's what proves the most popular, eggs are fried, I won't fanny around doing poached or scrambled of a morning and there's one big fat sausage each."

"Hallelujah," Vera says, nodding towards the image of the naked man and getting a look of contempt from Wilma before she disappears back through the fly screen.

The breakfast was satisfying and after I've sponged off a ketchup stain from Vera's blouse we head off into town once more. The day is bright and sunny, summer seems to have arrived in the northwest and we stand on the promenade looking at the beach. Families unpack blankets and buckets and spades as little ones toddle on the soft sand. A man settles his donkeys beside the sign advertising rides, and I think, my Victor would enjoy sitting on one.

We've got tickets for a matinee on the North Pier and make our way there, promising Mavis she can have a few goes on the slot machines while we all have a cuppa and a cake before the show. "Look at this," Vera says loudly, grabbing me by the arm and pointing at a shop window where there are sex aids displayed.

"Shocking," Doreen says.

"Is that a torch?" Mavis asks, pointing at an illuminated plastic penis.

"I don't think so," I say, adding, "but why it has a light on the top is beyond me." I turn around and Vera's disappeared, I look through the window display of vibrators and whips to see her deep in conversation with a woman behind the counter.

"What's she doing?" Mavis asks and I shrug.

"One of us needs to go inside and fetch her out," Doreen says, meaning me. I'm walking towards the doorway when Vera emerges, smiling but saying nothing.

The matinee is okay, nothing spectacular. The compere tells old jokes, the music is provided by a cabaret act that sings outdated songs and the magician's act leaves a lot to be desired. His tricks are very entertaining but his delivery is as fluid as treacle; his conversations with the audience would make excellent lullabies for fractious children.

We spend the afternoon walking around the pleasure beach, watching brave souls ride on contraptions that loop the loop and plummet like lemmings from a clifftop. Mavis once again has to be dragged away from penny machines – I wonder if she's got a gambling habit, I'll discuss it with Doreen when I get a chance – and for lunch, we sit on a bench with fish and chips. "There's something right about having a fish supper at the seaside," Vera says dipping a chip into tartare sauce.

"It's the sea air," Doreen says.

We all agree and I hand Vera a napkin to wipe her mouth.

"What shall we do next?" I ask them as I'm balling chip papers up and dropping them into a bin. "Do you fancy taking a look at the shopping centre?"

Doreen says she's going to head back to spend the afternoon with Wilma, "We need a catch-up."

"I might have a wander along the front," Mavis says and I spot her surreptitiously checking her purse for loose change.

"I'll come to the shops with you," Vera says. "I might get Mrs Khan a pair of oven gloves."

"Does she need oven gloves?"

"Who doesn't need oven gloves."

We all separate and Vera and I make our way to the Houndshill Centre. It's very clean, with lots of sparkling steel and a slightly risqué frieze on the wall. There are all the shops you'd find on a high street but without the pigeons and cigarette butts. I purchase a headband and socks for Lisa and Vera decides on a potato peeler and masher for Mrs Khan, the oven gloves forgotten for now.

We're used to shopping together and this time it's made pleasant by being away from familiar places, things that can stir up memories and people who know our business. We drop into a café for a frothy coffee and sitting at the window we watch people having a good time in the sunshine. Couples holding hands and children with smiles that are big enough to roll a ball inside.

"I like this, being away from Stoke for a while," Vera says.

"Me too. It's like having freedom without the responsibility of kids." I realise what I've said and apologise, but Vera shakes her head and places her hand on mine.

"I hardly ever think about not having children. It was something Emmett and I had got used to, but now …" she pauses and takes a sip of her drink, then says, "This isn't as nice as the ones in the bus station café back home."

"Do you fancy a piece of cake?" I point to a sign on the wall behind our table. "It says the owner has won awards for her cakes."

"That's no guarantee of excellence. I won a certificate for my fruit cake at the summer fayre in 1978, but it doesn't mean I'm in the same league as Mr Kipling." We laugh politely and then Vera continues, "I know it's silly but when I first found out that Emmett had died, I started to blame myself for having never given him a child. I hate that there's nothing left of him to continue on, and now there's not even a speck of dust to say he was once here."

"You'll always have your memories."

"Memories don't keep you warm at night, or make you toast and a runny egg for breakfast."

"I guess not …" I don't know what else to say. I'm lost, it feels like I'm reading a book written in a language that I don't understand, and the strange words just wash over me, meaning nothing, adding to my confusion.

"Do you mind if we stop talking about this?" I nod and she gives me a sad smile. "I want to be cheerful while we're here, I can always pick up the dropped stitches of sadness when I get home." It's my turn to smile as Vera says, "Go on, let's try a slice of their award-winning cake."

***

"I enjoyed last night," Doreen says as we board the coach home. "I don't even feel guilty about having had more than one drink."

"I think you had more than a couple; you were singing that Altered Images song, 'I Could Be Happy,' all the way back to Wilmas.

"I don't know the words to that song,"

"And don't we know it," Vera says.

"Or the tune," Mavis adds.

"All in all, I think it's been a nice breakaway. I just hope Len hasn't left a sink full of dishes for my return."

On time, the coach leaves Blackpool and Vera almost instantly falls asleep. I sit looking through the window, I'm in a reflective mood, as we move between the flat green spaces either side of the M55 and I think back to everything that's happened lately. Mavis seems to have got over Gerry's indiscretion and I think her close friendship with Doreen will help her to move on without him. Doreen will always be a little spiky, however, it's hard not to like her. She may be a stickler for rules and respectability, but sometimes that's what you need when life brings a problem to your door.

What can I say about Vera, she'll need more support from me over the coming weeks, but she's tough and she's got Mrs Khan to look after now, and of course me. Vera has always been my biggest supporter and I know if one day I need her to prop me up, she'll be there; possibly covered in biscuit crumbs, but I wouldn't have her any other way. Our friendship is free and costs nothing more than time. It's more precious than breathing, more fascinating than the universe and receiving it is more rewarding than any of our desires.

Back in Tunstall, we're walking home from the bus stop, both agreeing that the break was worth it. Vera says, once again thinking of someone other than herself, "At least it took Mavis's mind off her husband's shenanigans."

At Vera's front door, she fumbles in her bag for her keys and I say, "There is one thing I've been meaning to ask," she looks at me quizzically. "What did you say to the woman in the sex shop on the seafront?" Vera reaches into her handbag takes out a paper bag and hands it to me.

"I got this for my sister." I look inside and remove a tin whistle. I wrinkle my forehead in confusion and Vera turns it over so I can read that up the barrel is printed the words, 'Irishmen love a good blow.'

THE END

This mini novella is a prequel set in 1982 as a setting and character introduction to the novel, 52 Weeks, set in The Potteries in 2010 and released in January 2024. If you have enjoyed reading this sign up for Barry's Book Club mailing list for news and free books at **www.barrylillie.com**

Read on for a sneak look at chapter one of 52 Weeks.

Chapter One: 52 Weeks. Preview

~ Dr Chopra ~

Friday, 5 March 2010
I shall die earlier than I previously expected. My best prognosis is twelve months, that's fifty-two weeks, three hundred and sixty-five days and can you credit it, we're not even in a leap year.

***

"It is with regret that I have to inform you that the cancer has returned," Dr Chopra had said from behind the safety of his desk. "But it's not as straightforward as before." He looked uncomfortable and glanced down at the keyboard in front of him.

I guess delivering bad news never gets easier.

The outcome of my consultation was that my breast cancer, which was in remission up until a recent check-up had returned. When I say returned there's a small lump in my armpit that minor surgery can deal with but the worrying thing is there's now a tumour in my brain.

Dr Chopra's dark brown eyes seem to soften and become a milky colour. (Caffe-latte I imagine Lisa would call it.) "I'd like to be honest with you Mrs Bickerstaff." Len put his hand on my knee and I nodded my head, an indication that I was happy for him to be frank. "Metastatic breast cancer in the brain is extremely rare and so it currently has no cure, some treatments can help to control it, meaning people can live longer."

"How much longer?" I whisper.

"It's not an exact science. On average, the median survival rate from diagnosis is three to six months but with treatment it is possible to extend this to twelve months."

The room fell silent. Three pairs of eyes darted from one face to another until Dr Chopra spoke again. "I'm very sorry."

I said nothing.

"Mrs Bickerstaff, do you understand everything that I've said?"

"Yes, Doctor, but ask me again in a few weeks when the new tumour's taken hold."

***

This morning, I've been awake for what seems like hours, but in reality, is just minutes. Yesterday's conversation is hula-hooping in my consciousness, every word fastened to my memory like discarded chewing gum to a pavement. I slide a foot out of the duvet and wriggle my toes around like five, fat, fleshy thermometers assessing the temperature of the room. Deciding it's too chilly to get out of bed, my foot is returned to the warmth inside. Just then, as if in an attempt to warm me further, a rush of hot air brushes against my leg. Len has silently broken wind. Two seconds later, out of the top of the duvet, the aroma of physiologically recycled lamb tikka emerges. I know I should get out of bed and escape this assault on my olfactory system, but I'm unable to. I'm not physically incapable, just emotionally.

My mind skitters back to the hospital visit yesterday.

***

As we'd walked along the harshly lit hospital corridor, every earlier visit played in my head, fuzzy at the edges like an ancient videotape. That first uneasy appointment and examination by a junior doctor. The second for a discussion with a consultant, (things must be bad I had thought). Then the letter arrived, booking me in to start treatment.

"Do you know how many times we've been here in the past eighteen months?" Len said, pulling me back into the present. I shrug and shake my head. "Forty-two ... Forty-two trips. If we didn't have our free bus passes that would have amounted to £403.20. We spent less than half that on our honeymoon."

"I'm surprised you can remember that far back," I replied. "Five days on Anglesey in a caravan."

Back in the day, that was considered upmarket."

"Upmarket," I said. "Five days of drizzle and an unstable caravan."

"There was nowt wrong with that caravan."

"It was positively dangerous, every time you got amorous, I'm sure it moved a few feet closer to the gas bottle store."

Len laughed, "That could've been explosive."

"Good job when it came to sex, you were more of a sparkler than a rocket then."

Smiling, he hugged me publicly, something he rarely did, then said, "We'll be okay, you and me."

"We always have been," I told him, "Now stop mauling me you daft tray-cloth, and let's get the bus home."

Len, bless him, had tried his best to change the mood. Drinks in the Wedgwood Arms, a pint of brown ale for him and a Dubonnet and lemonade for me. "Queen's favourite tipple," he said, putting his pint glass down and wiping his mouth with the back of his hand.

"What, brown ale?"

"No, you daft beggar. Dubonnet."

"Oh."

Our drinks were followed by a visit to the Rose of Kashmir and we ate our dinner in silence. I liked the companionable calm, it meant we didn't have to talk about what had happened, or what was going to happen.

***

So now I'm in bed with a flatulent husband, and staring at the clock, willing the second hand to go backwards in a futile attempt to delay the foreseeable when there's another rumble beneath the duvet. I take that as my cue to get up.

The kitchen is cold, always has been. The extension tagged onto the back of the terrace not having enough room for both fitted units and a radiator. However, as with most houses in our street, there's always room for a dog basket. Cupping my morning brew, I watch as the dog squats in the backyard, not a pleasant sight, but one that oddly makes me feel alive. It doesn't matter what's going on in my life, the dog will still need feeding, emptying and cleaning up after.

Up until eighteen months ago when I had my surgery, my life – in my opinion – was quietly normal. I had no great plan, no agenda, in fact, it could be said that I've always been one of life's plodders. Human ballast, giving stability to the world around me. School led to a job in a potbank, where I met Len. This in turn led to marriage, kids and furniture on a repayment plan.

My husband, Len. God love him, is not, and has never been by any stretch of the imagination a sex symbol. He's more of your paint-splashed slippers and roll-ups sort of a man. We'll have been married forty-four years, in June. Most of those years have been happy, a few sad. Several monotonous, and thankfully, less than a handful have been downright miserable. We've created two wonderful children. I use the term, 'we' loosely, as Len's contribution was over faster than an Olympic sprinter with Crohn's disease. One minute I was sipping a cherry brandy at the local club and the next I was in the doctor's surgery clutching a jam jar filled with pee.

Although my life has been what I'd call, average, it could never be said to have been mundane. I may never have won tickets to the *Britain's Got Talent* final or set up my own tinned mackerel business, But my life has been rich in many other ways, and I did once stand behind the Potteries TV personality Anthea Turner in a post office.

I think most people would welcome an opportunity to reflect upon their life, I, however, don't. I don't want to wallow in the past, because life is about moving forward, not reflecting. I can still thread a needle without the need for spectacles, mash potatoes by hand and bend down far enough to cut my toenails.

It's just my left breast that's no longer there.

Glossary

Oatcake: Not to be confused with the crisp Scottish oatcake, Staffordshire oatcakes are a regional speciality of The Potteries and North Staffordshire. Usually eaten for breakfast with traditional breakfast fare, bacon, sausages, egg, cheese etc. The soft oatmeal pancakes are filled and rolled and served usually with tomato ketchup or brown sauce. Ask any 'Stokie' and they'll tell you they are the food of the gods.

Pot Bank: A pot bank is a factory where china and clay products are made, both dinnerware and giftware.

Cup Handler/Fettler: A fettler is a person working with dried clay products that have raised seams from the inside of the mould. To fettle is the practice of removing the seam. Cup handlers attach and sponge the handle to create a smooth surface on the china before it goes for the first firing. This work like cup handling was mostly completed by women in the industry.

Hanley: The city of Stoke on Trent is made up of six towns, (despite Arnold Bennett thinking that 'five' was more euphonious than the word 'six'). Hanley is the largest town and the main shopping/commercial of The Potteries' six towns.

Duck: This is a colloquial phrase used when addressing people in The Potteries, used in much the same way as 'love,' 'mate,' 'babe' etc. It has no gender and both men and women use it to address each other. E.G. At ow rate duck. (translation: How are you love?)

Backsies: The traditional thoroughfare running behind rows of terraced houses, also known up north as a ginnel or alleyway.

If you have enjoyed this mini-book, tell your friends and/or go to Amazon or Goodreads to write a review or simply just a star rating.

Your support is much appreciated.
Barry.

Printed in Great Britain
by Amazon